An Answer to a Tent Prayer

An Answer to a Tent Prayer

Tweakings and Tappings II

Suzanne Wachs Jones

Cover Illustration designed and drawn by Elizabeth Jones

Published 2020 KDP

Table of Contents

Dedication ix

Forward xi

Tent Prayers...xiii

An Answer to a Tent Prayer 1

Known by Your Fruit 7

Pancakes...12

Quarantined 17

Christmas Eve...22

Sandpaper People...27

Mooooooove On 32

Too Tired to Sleep 37

Almost Normal 42

Jackson and the Phone....................................46

Karen Revisited 53

Be Still..58

Miserable 62

October 2 66

Car Seat Christianity 72

Spiritual Firewalls 77

I Read This Book Once 82

Surely Lord You Don't Mean Me 86

The "Rightness" in Wrong Words 90

Putting Mommy to Shame........................93

Changing My Tune 99

Daughter 103

I Was Blind 106

Inferno Dragons 110

Reminders in the Sky 114

Joy to the World 120

He Healed Them All........................124

Last Minute Forgiveness 128

He Walked on Water 133

Always a Teacher........................138

I Know You Hear Us 143

Dedication

To Steve, Jackson, Elizabeth
and Emeline...all my love

To Heather Baker, for all the
editing help (again!)

To Val, for the title suggestion

To all who have encouraged
me to continue to write...
my thanks!

Forward

This book is collection of stories written over the span of several years. Some of the stories were written very recently, some as far back as five years ago. They are not in any sequential order. It is my hope that they offer some encouragement to you as you read them.

Happy reading!

Suzanne Wachs Jones
December 2020

Tent Prayers

"But Jesus said, 'Let the children come to Me. Don't stop them! For the Kingdom of Heaven belongs to those who are like these children.'"
Matthew 19:14 (NLT)

One afternoon not too long ago while we were in the living room, my three-year-old daughter made an out of the blue announcement. "I want 12 more babies! 10 boys and 2 girls!" Before I could say anything, she said "I'm gonna pray about it!" and hopped off the loveseat into the bedsheets and chairs tent the kids had been playing in and prayed.

In very simple words, and with a great deal of sincerity, "Dear God, I want 12 more babies. Ten boys and 2 girls. Amen."

And that was it. She jumped up and was on to the next thing.

Now, I am 42, have a son and a daughter, and last year had two miscarriages in 7 months, both after normal ultrasounds. The resulting surgery from the last one landed me in the ER with an overnight stay in the hospital.

It will take the hand of God moving for me to have another child.

But that is not what struck me about Elizabeth's prayer.

There were other things.

The first was that her first step, her first course of action was to pray. She didn't talk to anyone else (including her mother!), she talked to God. Now, she is just three and her circle is a *tad bit* limited, but, she spoke first to God about her desires. I do not mean to say that we shouldn't talk to our Godly friends and family. I believe we should. I believe that God puts these people in our lives for reasons. He speaks through them many times. But they should not be the first place we turn. I have, and am grateful for, the Godly men and women that He has put in my life. They have been and continue to be a source of comfort, wisdom and inspiration for me. But God should still be the first one I speak to.

Another thing that struck me about her prayer was the simplicity of it. No fancy words, no begging, no pleading, no bargaining, no cajoling, just her request. Just her desire. In plain and simple words, laid out before the One Who can do something about it.

I wonder sometimes why I don't do that more often. Just talk to Him the way I talk to my best friends. Sometimes a quick text to or from one of them speaks volumes. And a quick word or moment with Him can make a huge difference, too.

 Again, I know my daughter's prayers are more simple because she is so young. But she said what she needed to say. That was it. Of course, my friends and I wouldn't have the relationships we have if we hadn't spent lots of time together and if we didn't have in depth, long conversations, but we don't have to do that *all the time*. Same way with the Lord. Each time we speak, it doesn't have to be big fancy five-dollar words that take 30 minutes to say.

The other thing that stuck with me was that after she presented her request to God, she got up and moved on. She didn't get back up and moan and groan about it. She didn't get up and mope. She got up, and moved on. She took her request to Him and left it with Him.

All this to say that the way she prayed, the attitude in which she prayed, made me stop and think, and re-examine my prayer life. I think I could take a lesson from my little one...take everything to Him, take it to Him first, and leave it with Him.

The faith of a child.

Thanks, Elzie.

An Answer to a Tent Prayer

"He is the One you praise; He is your God, who performed for you those great and awesome wonders you saw with your own eyes."
Deuteronomy 10:21 (NIV)

While working on compiling these pieces into my first book, I have been rereading them, trying to catch all my missed commas, extra spaces, and incomplete thoughts. Many of the pieces I haven't read in a long time...some since I wrote them. It has been interesting to read them again, especially given the time that has elapsed since writing many of them.

The other day I read one called "Tent Prayers." It is about my daughter Elizabeth's desire to be a big sister and how she prayed about it. (In her little living room tent.) In the piece, I wrote *"I am 42, have a son and a daughter and last year had two miscarriages in 7 months, both after normal ultrasounds. The resulting surgery from the last one landed me in the ER with an overnight stay in the hospital. It will take the hand of God moving for me to have another child."*

I had to set the story aside after reading that statement and take a few long, slow breaths.

Because sitting on the floor playing with blocks is proof of the hand of God moving.

Our miracle baby girl was born last year.

Born to parents both WAY OLDER than the typical parent...me, a woman age 44, and my husband, age older than me.

We were *by far* the oldest patients on the labor and delivery floor of the hospital. But I will guarantee that we were also among the most excited.

I thought we were finished. I thought there was no way we would have another child. I was too old. The risk was too high. The odds were too long.

But God had other plans.

It was, for me, a looonnnggg pregnancy. Particularly a long first trimester. Actually, long until the time that I could feel her movements. Every time we went to the doctor prior to that, I was a mess. I've always been an emotional kind of person and the many trips to the OB during that time were nerve-wracking for me, to say the least.

It was as if I was on an emotional roller coaster. Nervous, excited, anxious...down right scared. I tried not to be a total basket case on the drive to the doctor's office, but often I did not succeed in that. I would go from feeling terribly nervous and anxious to feeling an overwhelming sense of relief when the doppler picked up her heartbeat. I cried every single time.

It was exhausting.

I tried not to worry. I tried not to fret. I knew I was doing all that I could do to ensure a safe pregnancy and a healthy baby. But it was So. Hard.

A few weeks prior to her due date, I was sitting in the swing in our side yard when the limb the swing was attached to broke. Down went the swing, down I went, and down the limb came. Right onto me. Mercifully Steve was at home and outside. We called the doctor and got to the office in record time.

I cried and prayed the whole way. But she was fine.
Totally unhurt.

We were scheduled to have her arrive on a set day,
but she had other plans. After two days of off-and-
on contractions, things began to move to the point
that we knew it was time to go to the hospital. So,
after getting our two older children taken care of,
we had another fast drive to my OB and hospital.
An hour away under normal circumstances. Not an
hour away that night.

Long story short, she arrived several days ahead of
schedule.

And she was perfect.

Beautiful.

I think she still is. My little baby is now over a year
old and walking. Babbling, smiling, and hollering
every now and then. God blessed our family with
this beautiful little girl. I don't know why He chose
to do so. I don't begin to understand His timing. I
have tried to think about the things I learned (or at
least got another lesson in) during the whole
process. Trust. Letting go of worry. Faith. Letting
go of worry. Belief that God will give me what I

need to handle whatever situation comes along. Letting go of worry.

Did I mention letting go of worry?

The Bible is full of examples of God working in ways we don't expect and in ways that can only be His handiwork...His hand moving and directing things as only He can.

I see this in my life.

Again and again.

Time after time.

I have seen "with my own eyes," as the Scripture from Deuteronomy says, God perform many "great and awesome wonders."

I saw Him answer a prayer offered by a three-year-old under a card table with some old blankets thrown across it.

And I am grateful, SO GRATEFUL, that I can hold and love one of the greatest and most awesome wonders He has ever worked in my life.

An answer to a tent prayer.

Known by Your Fruit

"Yes, just as you can identify a tree by its fruit, so you can identify people by their actions."
Matthew 7:20 (NLT)

Just a few days ago I was doing something I have said I was going to stop doing...mindlessly scrolling on Facebook. I try very hard not to be on it for long periods of time, but I am guilty of checking it almost every day. On one hand, it's a great way to see how everyone is doing, how fast kids are growing and to stay in touch with family and friends who live far away.

But on the other hand, five minutes can quickly turn into 45. Time that I should be spending doing something else.

Anything else really.

This particular day I saw a repost of an article written by a Christian woman about child-rearing. The title caught my eye and I read it. All in all, it was a decent article, nothing truly earth-shattering, but a good reminder of some basic principles.

But what really stood out to me was the person who posted it and her comments. She had put a comment under it about things she was doing with her kids that went along with the article and she finished with a "churchy/religious" type statement.

Before I go any further with my rant, let me first say that I do not know this person very well. I have spoken with her a few times and I see her from time to time, but to say I really know her would not be accurate. I write what I am about to write not to judge her relationship with God, because that is not for anyone to do, but to simply make a point and to remind myself of a few things.

This person puts up a lot of Christian type posts. She puts up prayer requests, reposts articles, etc. There is nothing at all wrong with that. But what jumps out to me is that I see no evidence of Christianity in her life outside of Facebook. Nothing that would make me think "There is a Christian." She doesn't go around kicking puppies or stealing from the elderly, but there is little evidence, at least in what I see, that would identify her as a believer.

The best way to say what I am thinking is that she talks a good game, but there is no action associated with the talk. There does seem to be a great deal of *inaction*.

And again, she may have a wonderful Christian life. I don't know. I just know that what I see is a mismatch in actions and words.

After reading her post and climbing down off my high horse, I began to wonder if anyone thinks the same about me.

I wonder how many people look at me and think "She claims to be a Christian, but her life sure doesn't look like it!" or "I didn't expect a Christian to act like that!" or "I thought she went to church!" or "I can't believe a Christian would say such a thing!"

Scripture tells me that I will be known by my fruit. In essence, if I'm right in my relationship and walking daily (at least trying to walk daily) with God, and growing in my faith, then I will produce good fruit. I will act Christlike if I am walking with Christ. When I am not walking daily with Him, my actions show it.

When I'm being rotten, that is the kind of fruit I'll produce. Rotten, nasty fruit. I can see it myself when I get away from reading my Bible. I don't feel right. I don't show the patience I should, or have the right attitude with people.

If it is obvious to me when I'm not right in my walk, then I am sure it is obvious to other people. I think that the Scripture verse from Matthew leaves no doubt. It says "you CAN identify people by their actions." I have heard it said before that "You may be the only Bible some people ever read." I am afraid that sometimes the Bible I show isn't an accurate reflection of the real Bible.

One lesson here for me is that people *do* look, people *do* watch, and people *do* form opinions. Some may even form part of their opinion of Christians, and Christianity in general, based on my actions and inactions...whether good or bad. While it is true that no one can judge another's relationship with the Lord, it is also true that I can point people toward Christ or away from Him with my behavior.

Staying "plugged in" to Him, and in step with Him, is vital to my own spiritual life and to my witness as well.

The other lesson is...I really need to stay off social media.

Pancakes

"So encourage each other and build each other up, just as you are already doing."
I Thessalonians 5:11 (NLT)

A few years ago, I began running for exercise. Again. Running is something I have done off and on since high school. I had gotten into a pretty good routine, for me anyway, when we found out that Miracle Baby was on the way. Pretty soon after that running became impossible, so, I gave it up.

About six months after she was born, I joined a few friends from church on their Saturday morning jogs. Two people in this group had recently done a half marathon, so keeping up with them was quite the challenge. I wasn't very fast and my distances weren't impressive, but I did enjoy being outside and the benefits that came along with being in better shape. That December, we ran in the local 5K. They were out of sight before I finished the first stretch. But I finished the race which was my goal.

Since December, I've worked on increasing my distances, little bit by little bit. Slowly. Slowly. Slowly.

About two months ago my friend Kristina, who is one of the Saturday morning runners, sent a text message to the rest of us about a race she had found. There was a 4 miler and a 10 miler. I looked at the information and texted back "Yes! The four miler looks great!" thinking that would push me a little bit and would be the longest race I have ever run.

To my surprise (and horror) she wrote back "No… we're gonna do the 10 miler!"

Kristina is one of those people who can run for days on end and it doesn't look like it bothers her at all. She makes it look effortless. I, on the other hand, huff and puff and pant and drag myself along. She can run circles around me. And, as we have built up our distances, she has. She will get ahead of me and then loop back to where I am struggling, chanting "Pancakes! Pancakes! Pancakes!" and occasionally "Blueberry syrup!"

See, I have decided that if I get through this ten-mile race and can still walk, I'm going to IHOP and stuff myself with pancakes smothered in blueberry syrup. Kristina knows this is my plan and uses it to motivate and encourage me to keep going when I really want to stop.

This past week in Sunday School we had a lesson on contentment. Some of the verses dealt with encouragement and endurance. I thought about how her encouragement (and that of the others who run and walk with me) is essential to keep me going when things get tough during our training runs.

I need their encouragement when I run. I need to hear "Just a little bit more. We're almost there! You can do it!"

And I need encouragement in other areas of life, too.

I need someone to come beside me and run with me. I need someone to speak the right words to help me keep going, especially when life gets challenging. I need someone to notice that I'm falling behind and circle back to check on me. I need someone to say "We're almost there" and put themselves in the race with me. I need someone to remind me that something great is ahead if I just keep plugging along.

I've been blessed to have people who have done that in the past and friends who do it today. So many of them exemplify the verse from I Thessalonians. They excel at encouraging and building other people up. Paul reminds us to do just that, but finishes the verse by saying "Just as you are already doing." I'm afraid that oftentimes people would not be able to say that about me. I have good intentions but life gets busy and I forget to call. Or forget to send the text. Or the email. And ashamedly, sometimes I forget to pray for people.

Thinking about the race and the verses from Sunday School, I am reminded how important it is to be the encourager.

It's a reminder to myself to pay attention to others.

To look for times when they might need encouragement.

To look for areas in which someone might need encouragement.

And once I know, loop back around and run alongside them.

And remind them that their own personal plate of blueberry syrup covered pancakes might be just around the corner.

Quarantined

"And let us not neglect our meeting together, as some people do, but encourage one another, especially now that the day of His return is drawing near."
Hebrews 10:25 (NLT)

This is day number "I'm not even sure what" of the COVID-19 quarantine. School has been cancelled for weeks now and there is no telling when/if we will go back. We have hardly ventured out of the house. Everything has been disrupted. Church services have been cancelled. Life as we know it has come to a screeching halt.

Some church members who are much more technologically advanced than I am have begun to broadcast our service online. Our youth minister has started a Facebook group for the church so we can do our best to stay in touch.

All that is great...but it's not the same as being at church.

I miss church.

Other than when my children were born, I can't think of a time that I missed more than two Sundays in a row.

I've missed the occasional Sunday here and there when I've been sick or one of the kids has been sick. And once in a while when we get more than a dusting of snow here in NC, services are cancelled.

But this is different.

Church is called off for the foreseeable future. No Wednesday night service. No mission groups. No Ladies Chorus practice. No Sunday School. No corporate worship services. And contrary to good Baptist doctrine, no meals together.

It is weird.

And I don't like it.

I didn't realize just how much being there meant to me until now. Sure, those rare Sundays that I have missed made my week feel somewhat off, but this is *beyond* off.

As a family we have watched a local church broadcast every Sunday since our services have been cancelled. The same one we watch when one of us is home sick. It is a great service. They have spliced in segments of their orchestra and choir from previous Sundays. They have a moment with the children's minister. They have hymns that we can sing together at home. And, of course, a sermon.

And now our church has online services, which is wonderful. But it is not the same as being there in person with other believers.

I am an introvert by nature, not given to much talking in big groups. But I need to be around people. Too much alone time makes me a little nuts.

We are doing our best to comply with the recommendations to stay home, venturing out only to restock the refrigerator. Avoiding unnecessary contact with people...even staying away from family that we don't live with. Thankfully we live in a rural area, so we can be outside without being in contact

with other people. My kids can ride their bikes,
jump on the trampoline and play with the dog out in
the open. I can get my running in by making loops
in our quarter mile driveway.

But I find myself missing social interaction.

I think social interaction is part God's design for us.

Hebrews tells us that we should not forsake meeting
together as brothers and sisters in Christ. Humans
were not made to be alone. In Genesis we see that
Adam, even though surrounded by the perfection of
God's new creation, was lonely. Until God created
Eve. In her was someone to share things with,
someone to talk to, someone to experience the
wonders of the world with. Companionship...In
short, just to *be* with.

This "being together" is important in a spiritual
sense, too. I try to read my Bible every day (some
days sadly I don't). I pray every day. But the
encouragement and support I get from my brothers
and sisters in Christ is *crucial*. There is the
accountability, too. No one likes to be corrected,
but sometimes it is necessary. If I'm off in
something and don't see it, I need someone to
gently and lovingly point it out to me. To redirect

me, help me get back on course. And then check on me to make sure I haven't slipped off course again.

I think that is what Hebrews is telling us. We *need* each other. We were made to be together.

To worship together.

To sing together.

To be together.

When this is all over, I think a good old-fashioned Baptist meal is in order.

Stay safe.

Christmas Eve

"And then He told them, 'Go into all the world and preach the Good News to everyone.'"
Mark 16:15 (NLT)

Today is Christmas Eve.

We have been counting down the days in our house for a while now. At some point during the day - everyday - for the past few weeks the question has come up "How many days til Christmas Eve?" followed by "Then only fill in the blank more days until Christmas?"

My children are excited about it this year. Actually, they are excited about it every year. So am I. I think I enjoy Christmas more as an adult than I did

as a child. Not that I didn't enjoy it as child. I did.
My Momma and Daddy always made Christmas
special. My brother and I were always up
early...even when we became teenagers. I
understand now how little sleep my parents got
many Christmas Eve nights.

Our Christmas traditions have evolved over the
years as we have gotten older and people have been
added to our family.

But one Christmas tradition that has remained for
the whole of my life is Christmas Eve at Uncle
Norman and Aunt Mary Lea's house. Actually, I
think the tradition started sometime in the 1940's.

Every Christmas Eve the Brown family gathers at my
Uncle's house to visit, eat, talk, eat, laugh, eat,
reminisce and eat some more. Uncle Norman is my
grandfather Papa Brown's younger brother. The last
of the 9 siblings. He and his wife Aunt Mary Lea live
in the house that the Brown siblings grew up in. I
knew all but one of them. Most lived close to the
homeplace and were there on Christmas Eve.

As a child the event seemed huge to me. We used
to draw names and exchange gifts. In my memory
the entire front room was filled with gifts, and the
entire house was filled with people. I would guess

that there used to be upwards of 80 people there. The numbers have fluctuated through the years as people have gotten married, new Browns have been born and older family members passed on.

But Christmas Eve has always been there.

We live a good 45 minutes away from Uncle Norman and Aunt Mary Lea's house, but it matters not. I want to go, even if we can only be there for a short amount of time.

So, today I was in the kitchen making some snacks to take down there when Momma called.

She was calling to tell me that the Christmas gathering has been cancelled this year. Uncle Norman is sick.

So, change of plans.

I'm sad.

I could count on my two hands, maybe even one, the number of Christmas Eves that I have not made the trip to the small town of Bennett to spend at least a few hours surrounded by my extended family, many of whom I rarely get to see.

Something will be missing from my Christmas this year. It can't be helped and hopefully we can have a family gathering soon when "Unk" is all better. But this year will for sure seem different without the trip to the Brown homeplace.

What I was hit with as I thought about how different my night will feel tonight, with the "something's missing," is that there are countless people around me celebrating Christmas without really knowing what, or why, they are celebrating. They are missing more in their Christmas than a family gathering.

They have trees, lights, presents, all that good stuff. Santa will find them tonight for sure. But they are missing the key to it all.

They are unaware of, or unconcerned with, the real reason for Christmas.

The birth of Jesus.

I wonder if people who have Santa but no Savior feel a void.

I wonder if people who have presents but no Presence feel a little hollow.

I wonder if people who have lights on a tree but don't know the Light of the World feel like something is missing.

And what have I done about it?

Too often the answer is nothing.

I have friends - good friends - who do not share my beliefs. Who do not believe in the virgin birth, the angel's announcement, who don't believe that the birth of Jesus was anything more than the birth of another good man who shared some good teachings while He was here.

At this most special time of the year, I am often too wrapped up in the baking, shopping and planning of my own celebrations that I don't make the effort to share what I'm really celebrating. I don't have to go far to "go into all the world" as Jesus told us to do.

I could start right down the road.

Maybe next year the trip to Uncle Norman's won't be missing for me, and my prayer is that the real Reason for the Season won't be missing for others.

Sandpaper People

"You have heard that it was said, 'You shall love your neighbor and hate your enemy.' But I say to you, love your enemies and pray for those who persecute you, so that you may be sons of your Father who is in heaven. For He makes His sun rise on the evil and on the good, and sends rain on the just and on the unjust. For if you love those who love you, what reward do you have? Do not even the tax collectors do the same? And if you greet only your brothers, what more are you doing than others? Do not even the Gentiles do the same?" **Matthew 5:43-48 (ESV)**

"It doesn't hurt to be nice" Steve said.

Again.

Because once again, I was unloading my frustrations on him after dealing with a "sandpaper person" – one of those people who rubs me the wrong way. This person is the sandpaperiest person I know. In fact, I would go so far as to say that she is the sandpaperiest person I have ever run across.

I don't like her.

One bit.

I'll call her "Karen."

I don't have to deal with Karen every day, which is good for my blood pressure. Because often when I do have to deal with her, I leave the situation ready to explode.

But I can't completely avoid dealing with her. Without going into too much detail lest I reveal her identity, it's not possible to avoid all dealings with her.

She doesn't listen to me, which is one of my biggest pet peeves.

She doesn't pay attention to things I think she should pay attention to. Things that sometimes wind up affecting me. And that annoys me.

So, after this last run in with her, I was unloading all my irritable thoughts and telling my husband what I *really* want to do in my dealings with her.

It would not have made my grandparents proud.

Steve is gracious to listen and offer sound counsel. He doesn't operate off the raw emotion that Karen brings out in me. Which is good. Because usually I need to be talked back into my senses.

Not that I would really do or say any of the things going around in my red-haired head. But I am a little ashamed at how good the idea of unloading on her makes me feel.

A little.

Often after listening to another one of my verbal tirades, Steve will say, "Yes, but it doesn't hurt to be nice." He's right. (Most of the time.)

But guess what dawned on me yesterday after I finished my ranting?

God loves her.

And Jesus died for her.

And that realization was uncomfortable for me.

I don't like her. But *He* loves her. Enough to die for her.

I don't usually want to do anything to be nice and helpful, but Christ offered His life for her. His life! I don't even want to offer a smile.

Thinking about that made me feel very ashamed. Because honestly, most of the time I think I'm a better person than she is. I think, in some ways, I deserve a little more mercy and grace than she does. But you know what?

I'm not.

And I don't.

Am I not called - commanded even - to be Christlike? To strive to be more so every single day? And yet, I let this person bother me again and again. Again and again I think unpleasant thoughts about her.

Jesus instructed us in the Sermon on the Mount to "Love your enemies and pray for those who persecute you." I know in the logical part of my brain - which doesn't get near the amount of exercise as the emotional part of my brain does - that she doesn't set out to persecute me. We are different, we see the world differently and we react to the world differently. Those differences are part of what fuel my displeasure.

Karen has said she is a Christian, which makes her my sister in Christ. Another troublesome realization.

I'm told to pray for her.

I don't.

I'm not responsible for her behavior. But I am responsible for mine. What would happen if every time I started to think about what a pain she is, I offered a prayer? And in my prayers, I prayed not only for her, but also for my attitude?

My bet is that I would begin to see a change in my attitude. Maybe a bump up in my patience level. And maybe a touch of understanding towards her.

And maybe a lowering of my blood pressure when I do interact with her.

Mooooove On

"I tell you the truth, those who listen to My message and believe in God who sent Me have eternal life. They will never be condemned for their sins, but they have already passed from death into life."
John 5:24 (NLT)

A while back I was working my way through the book of John again, probably my favorite of the 4 gospels, when I ran across this verse.

I took a picture of the page in my Bible and sent it to my friend Janet along with a message about how timely I thought the verse was because I was struggling with guilt.

Again.

It isn't the first time.

Knowing me, it won't be the last.

Speaking only as a true friend can she said "Girl! Mooooove on! He has!" (The mooooo being a reference to a cow joke that we have been laughing about for almost twenty years now.)

That stuck with me.

I have mulled over what she said repeatedly. He has moved on.

God has moved on.

These little pieces that I write sometimes come to me several at a time and other times it seems I have dry spells for writing.

The past few weeks have been a dry period. A couple of times I have tried to write something, but the thoughts haven't really flowed.

My mind kept coming back to what Janet told me. And then, I felt a whisper in my spirit that said "I want you to think on this...to focus on this for a little bit."

I decided to look for Scripture describing God's forgiveness. Here are just a few of what I've found (all the italics are mine):

"Who is a God like You, who pardons sins and forgives the transgressions of the remnant of His inheritance? *You do not stay angry forever but delight to show mercy*." Micah 7:18

"I, even I, am He who blots out your transgressions, for My own sake and *remembers your sins no more*." Isaiah 43:25

"If we confess our sins, *He is just to forgive us our sins* and to cleanse us from all unrighteousness."   I John 1:9

"In Him we have redemption through His blood, *the forgiveness of our trespasses,* according to the riches of His grace." Ephesians 1:7

"Come now, let us reason together, says the Lord: though your sins are like scarlet, *they shall be as white as snow;* though they are red like crimson, they shall become like wool." Isaiah 1:18

"For *everyone* who calls on the name of the Lord will be saved." Romans 10:13

"As far as the east is from the west, so far does *He remove our transgressions from us*." Psalm 103:23

Know what all that means?

Those sins that I can't seem to forgive myself for are gone.

Taken away.

Removed.

No more.

God, because of Jesus, has removed them. **God** has removed them. God, who created everything, including me, has Himself removed the sins.

He remembers them no more.

Everyone who calls on the Lord will be saved. The sins are removed *by God* as far as the east is from the west. God delights in showing mercy.

The verse from John says that we have already passed into life. I think that has two meanings. Certainly it applies to the afterlife for those who are saved by the blood of Jesus. We will have eternal life. But the verb is in the past tense. We have *already* passed from death into life. I think it also applies here to life on earth. I have passed from death into life, eternally, yes but here as well. I need not worry about the mistakes of the past. I've asked God to forgive me and He has. I need to take Janet's advice and "mooooove on"...pass from the "death" that guilt brings and into the life that Christ promised.

There is no reason to let the past hinder the life that is here in the present.

God has forgiven.

God has cleansed.

God offers new life, new freedom in Christ.

I need only mooooove toward it.

Too Tired to Sleep

"Then Jesus said, 'Come to Me, all of you who are weary and carry heavy burdens, and I will give you rest.'"
Matthew 11:28 (NLT)

Today, the first Sunday after Christmas, is the first day in over a week that we haven't had somewhere to go, other than church this morning. It has been a good Christmas season, but to say it has been busy is an understatement.

We have had countless meals with family and friends and have enjoyed it all. But it has been tiring.

Today at lunch, Little Bit, who is roughly 20 months old, just about fell asleep at the table. I guess the last few days have finally caught up with her. When her Daddy picked her up to move her to the bed, she woke with a start. She spent the next 25 minutes in a full-blown toddler fit.

She trotted from room to room crying.

She picked up at least 4 different stuffed animals only to throw them back down.

I offered her a sippy cup, and then her bottle, only to have her shake her little curly haired head vehemently "No!"

Nothing satisfied her.

I called her name time and time again, quietly, trying to get her attention. I even tried picking her up several times, too, but she would throw her arms up in the air and slide out of my grip.

I knew she needed to rest, but getting her to do so was proving complicated.

Finally, she succumbed to sleep, having settled down next to me on the loveseat, her sippy cup slipping out of her little hand.

I sat beside her for a few minutes, rubbing her curls, soaking up being with her. And making sure she was really asleep before trying to move her, lest I wake her and the tantrum start again!

As I watched her sleep, I began to think about what she had done this afternoon. She had run away, time and time again, from what she needed. She had been so busy looking for something to help her that she missed the one thing that would have helped. She was making so much noise hollering that she couldn't hear me quietly calling her to rest.

I thought to myself how like her I am sometimes.

I stay busy. Who doesn't? As the mother of three, at three totally different stages of childhood and adolescence (ages 14, 7 and 20 months), I spend a great deal of time running here and there. We have Girls In Action and youth group at church. The 14-year-old and the 7-year-old both play basketball, but their schedules are different. They are at the same school, but with the older one's basketball practice ending a couple of hours after school ends, many days I make three trips to school. Throw in Tae-Kwon-Do a couple of times each week and basketball practice for the 7-year-old, and each week seems busier than the last.

Then we have Little Bit, who gets dragged to more events than I ever went to as a child. The poor girl has learned to catch short cat naps in the car between different functions.

I, apart from the kids, am busy myself with things I am involved in at church, school, and other places. Plus the normal duties of trying to run a household. Some days the laundry pile is high and the fridge supply is low.

None of these in and of itself is bad. Most in fact are very good. I want the kids to be involved in sports. It keeps them moving and develops all kinds of good characteristics. I want them to see their father and mother doing things at church, being involved, taking part, and contributing.

But I think sometimes I am like my toddler. Running from one thing to another...one event, one function, one meeting, to another.

And how often have I picked up something thinking it was what I needed only to realize, like Little Bit, that it didn't do the trick. Throw it down, look for something else. Repeat. Repeat.

How many times have I run from God's calling, thinking I could take care of myself? When in reality

He has what I needed all along. How often, like her, have I been too loud to hear the soft voice calling me to come to what I need.

Rest.

Quiet time with Him.

Time to not *do* anything, but just *be*.

Be still, quiet, and calm.

She woke up after a two-hour nap, happy and smiling.

I could take a lesson from her there too.

How much happier, calmer, and more at peace I would be if I would take the time to sit with my Father, let Him stroke my curls, and listen to Him whisper His love for me.

She has grinned the rest of the afternoon...happy as she can be.

Gives me something to shoot for.

Almost Normal

"The thief comes only to steal and kill and destroy. I came that they may have life and have it abundantly."
John 10:10 (ESV)

Today is June 12.

June 12, *2020*.

Day 6,580 of the COVID-19 quarantine.

Not really.

But there have been times during this "safe at home" period that have felt that way.

Today was a wonderful day. It has been hot this week here in NC. Hot and humid. Today was neither. It was somewhere in the low to mid 80's. Manageable humidity. One of the few glorious days during the summer when it is nice outside all day.

This morning I took my kids to an orchard a few miles down the road. It is open for "pick your own" berries. We have gone here in the past, pre-COVID-19, and enjoyed hay rides, slushies, stories and play time during their weekly Children's Time. Those things are not happening right now, but we can at least pick berries.

Two good friends from church also went. One friend had her children with her, who are virtually the same ages as my older two. We picked some beautiful berries and my children thoroughly enjoyed being in the same vicinity as their friends...something we haven't done in months.

After leaving the orchard we decided to stop at a new ice cream parlor on the way home. That was the icing on the cake.

The day had an almost normal feel to it.

I needed that.

We have not had it as rough as many other folks during the pandemic. We haven't been sick, haven't been confined indoors and haven't run out of toilet paper, the new gold standard.

But that doesn't mean that these haven't been challenging times.

I have missed being with other people. Being out. Eating out. Doing things that were our normal.

Sometimes it has been hard to be cheerful. I have tried...most of the time. But some of the time, I have failed. I've been grumpy, irritable and short tempered with my family, who - bless them - have been stuck at home with me.

There was such joy in the simple things we did today. Being outside. Talking with friends. Eating ice cream. Just seeing other people. Simple things.

I think in the past I have sometimes gotten so busy that I forget to see the joy in the everyday. And I think that doesn't bother the devil in the least. Jesus tells us that the devil has come to "steal, kill and destroy." My thinking is that if the evil one can't have the soul for eternity, he will do his best to steal, kill and destroy the joy that can be found here on earth.

I need to do my best not to let that happen. I need to get up each day focusing on what's good and what's right. I need to look for the joy in the everyday.

I can accept that things may not be exactly how I want them right now, and I don't have to like it, but I can do a better job of not letting those circumstances which I can do nothing about steal all the happiness out of my world.

When this is over, I hope I never again take for granted our church services, going to a local restaurant, seeing my Momma and Daddy whenever I wish, taking my kids somewhere they want to go, and many other things I am wishing I could do now.

I hope I never take for granted the joy that is here, everyday IN the everyday.

Jackson and the Phone

"The LORD is good to those who wait for Him, to the person who seeks Him."
Lamentations 3:25 (NASB)

A few weeks ago we did something I had not planned on doing for at least another year.

We got our son a cell phone.

Getting him a phone wasn't something I had planned to do before he was officially a teenager. He's close - only about 5 more months - but not quite there.

Not that he wasn't asking for one.

He was.

Often.

And with great perseverance.

My answer to him was always "You don't need one."

He didn't. More than likely he still doesn't.

But after a less than ideal experience at summer camp, I decided it might be time.

Jackson was excited about camp, and we were excited for him to go. This was the first time he had been old enough to go to youth camp with our church. It was held at a college in another state...a good 5-hour drive from home.

The day they left for camp, I took him to church and stayed until the van pulled out. He was ready! I was happy for him to have that experience.

That night, I awoke to the sound of my husband in the bathroom, sick.

Not good. Especially since within about 15 minutes of waking up, I was sick too.

Not sick like a small head cold with a cough. I mean SICK...miserably sick.

We passed the night in agony, then passed the morning in agony.

About mid-morning, things got worse. I got a text from Jackson's camp roommate and good friend saying "Jackson just got sick."

Really not good.

I called our youth minister (who was with Jackson) and spoke with him, then spoke with Jackson. He was running a fever and after talking with him and our youth minister, we decided it would be best to try to get him home.

The decision was the easy part. The actual logistics of that were complicated.

Neither my husband nor I could move very far from the bathroom.

And Jackson was more than 5 hours from home.

We finally got things worked out so that my parents could meet the youth minister's wife about halfway between camp and our house. Then they would bring him home. Not something I wanted to ask them to do, but our options were very limited.

There was no way I could drive and no way Steve could drive.

Long story short, he made it home, but it was an all-day event. I felt so bad for him. It was bad being sick myself, having my husband sick, and trying to take care of our 4-month-old, but it was torture to know he was not well and I was unable to care for him. I did my best to make him comfortable and take care of him when he did get home.

That was what finally broke my last bit of resistance to him having a phone. I could not get in touch with him directly and that was *really hard* on me while he was feeling so bad.

So, after everyone healed and hubby and I talked about the limitations that would be imposed on the phone, we decided to take the plunge. I had recently gotten a new phone and still had my old one. The plan was to take the old one back to the store, re-activate it and give it to Jackson.

He was more than enthusiastic about it.

But when we got there, they told us that since my phone was "so out of date" they were no longer supporting it on their network and we wouldn't be able to activate it.

Jackson went from excited to dejected in a matter of seconds.

While we were there, my husband (who had not upgraded his phone in about five years) began to look around. He found something he liked and decided it might be time to upgrade. The salesman then told us that they were running a promotion that if Steve bought the phone he was looking at, then we could get another (lower priced) model at no charge. We didn't share that with Jackson at the time.

We left the store that night to think about it, but did wind up going back the next day and getting Steve a new phone. In the process, we took advantage of the promotion and got Jackson a phone as well.

A new phone.

A much nicer, newer phone than my old one.

He was very disappointed when the original plan didn't work out, but unbeknownst to him something much better was coming that couldn't have happened if our first plan had worked.

The way things happened with Jackson and the phone is much like how things work in our lives sometimes. We have a plan, have a goal in mind and do all that we can to make it happen.

But God has something even better in mind, and to bring His plan to fruition, our plan has to fall by the wayside.

When this has happened to me, I'm often like Jackson was in the phone store. Sad, dejected. Wondering why my well-laid plans didn't work out like I thought they should. Then later when things work out in a better way, I marvel at how things are far better than I had anticipated.

I've heard it said that God has three answers to prayers: "Yes," "No" and "Wait...I've got something better for you."

God is good. God loves us. Scripture tells us that He wants to give us good things, that He wants to bless us.

Sometimes waiting on Him to move is hard. We want to take things into our own hands instead of waiting on God. Lamentations tells us "The LORD is good to those who wait for Him, to the person who seeks Him." Too often I don't wait for Him and I don't seek His counsel in all things. I move forward with my life, acting as if I'm the utmost authority on what is good for me.

Which could not be further from the truth.

Jackson now enjoys his new phone and can do much more with it than he ever could have done on my outdated phone.

Likewise, I could do so much more if I learned to wait on Him.

No phone app necessary.

Karen Revisited

"Always be humble and gentle. Be patient with each other, making allowance for each other's faults because of your love."
Ephesians 4:2 (NLT)

A few days ago I wrote about someone code named "Karen" and how this person gets on my nerves. My very last nerve.

I concluded my piece with my plan to pray for Karen, instead of fussing about her when I have to deal with her.

I thought it was a GREAT idea.

And I was feeling pretty good about myself.

Good job, Suzanne. Good Christian. Good.

Then no more than two hours after I wrote my piece about Karen (and while still patting myself on the back for being such a good Christian) I had a Karen encounter.

I guess God decided that it was time for me to put my new plan into practice.

Truthfully, I wasn't ready for that. I wanted to bask in my plan for a little while. Feel good about myself for making such a *good* decision. Keep congratulating myself for setting such a "Christian" goal. And honestly, I wanted to have time to prep for my next encounter with her, psych myself up. Get some prayers ready. Plan some good "insta-responses."

My inner two-year-old had a heyday with the timing.

No, no, no God! Not now! I don't want to be nice to her today. I want to wait. I want to be nice when I'm good and ready. Give me more time! Don't make me live up to it today!

But that's not what I'm called to do, is it?

I am called to be Christlike all the time. Not only when I've had a good night's sleep, not only when I'm feeling particularly generous, and certainly not only when I'm ready.

The verse from Ephesians tells me to "always" be humble and gentle. This is a very tough thing for me. The "always" part. Some days especially.

But the harder part of the verse for me is the second part: "Making allowance for each other's faults."

OFTEN, it's hard to make allowances for people. Especially her, someone that I have a history of aggravation with. It is hard for me to forgive someone who has wronged me in what I consider big ways, someone I feel I have a *right* to be angry with.

But you know what? God through Christ has forgiven me for all my sins.

For all my misdeeds.

For all my disobedience.

For all the times I've said something I shouldn't have said.

For the many more times I've thought something I shouldn't have thought, even if I somehow managed to stay in control of my tongue.

For all the times I've done something I shouldn't have done. When I didn't know it was wrong *and* when I did.

How do I do that for the little Karens and the big Karens in my life?

That's the third part of the verse:

"...because of your love."

I am no Biblical scholar but I take that to mean because of my love for Christ. Not my love for Karen, but my love for Him. He loves her. And because of my love for Him I should try my best to treat her as He would. To treat everyone as He would. My friends, my family, my acquaintances, and my Karens.

I should try to please Him in my words and in my actions.

All the time.

"His mercies begin afresh each morning."
Lamentations 3:23

God's mercies are new each day. Good thing.

I expect other people to show mercy to me, I should be willing to show mercy to others as well.

Because I'm sure I'm Karen to someone.

Be Still

He says, "Be still, and know that I am God;"
Psalm 46:10 (NIV)

My house is loud.

Loud because my children are talkers. To each other, to their friends, to their stuffed animals, to my husband and/or me, to no one in particular. Sometimes they take turns talking, sometimes they don't. When they are in "chatter mode" it is hard to think. I have told my husband many times that by the end of the day, I can't form a coherent thought in my head, let alone produce something intelligent to say.

They are active. They are happy. And I am thankful.

But there are times when I want to hold them.

Be still and hold them.

Be *silent* and hold them.

Not *do* anything. Just be still and hold them.

Soak up just being with them.

Love them.

I wonder how often God feels like that with me. Wonder how many times (in my prayer life in particular) God wants me to just be still. Be silent. And just be held.

I find it hard to be silent during my prayers; to listen for His voice instead of talking.

But on occasion, I do manage to get in that quiet place and sit. And be still. And soak up just being with Him. It feels good; comforting, rejuvenating. The Lord knew what He was saying (of course) when He encouraged us to "Be still."

There is a scene in the book <u>Sensible Shoes</u> by Sharon Garlough Brown in which one of the main characters envisions herself running in and out of the throne room of heaven bringing flowers to Jesus. Being busy, doing good works. Jesus finally gets her attention and says something to the effect of "The flowers are nice, but what I really want is to sit with you." (I'm paraphrasing.)

That scene really resonated with me. I can see myself needing to be told the same thing. Slow down. Put down your busy behavior. Sit. Soak up His presence. Soak up just being with Him. Come away and let Him recharge your soul.

It reminds me of the story of Mary and Martha from Luke 10. The Lord is at the home of Mary and Martha, and Martha is busy; preparing food, seeing to her guests, moving, doing.

Mary is not.

She is busy, but busy with something much more important.

Mary is busy sitting at the feet of Jesus, listening and learning.

Being still in the Presence of Jesus.

Too often I find myself on the Martha end of the spectrum. Busy doing what I think needs to be done instead of what ought to be done.

While certain things do have to be done everyday, Jesus reminds Martha that what Mary is doing is "needed," to quote Luke 10:42.

Be still.

Sit.

Listen.

And learn.

.

Miserable

"Father, if You are willing, take this cup from Me; yet not My will, but Yours be done."
Luke 22:42 (NIV)

Miserable.

There really is no other way to describe how I was feeling as I sat for what seemed like a very long time. I was listening to someone I didn't really know, talk about something I didn't know much about, for way longer than I cared to be sitting there.

The longer I sat there the more I felt like my brain was slowly losing its ability to function. My body was tired from being still and I'm pretty sure brain cells were dying with each passing minute.

I mentally checked out long before the session ended.

Several times I thought of getting up and leaving. Or getting up and pretending I needed a drink of water. But I didn't. I was proud of myself for not getting up. I didn't want to hurt anyone's feelings, especially not the people I was there to support.

But that didn't stop me from wanting to leave. Every minute that went by that I didn't get up to leave felt like a victory in perseverance.

When it was finally over and I could head home, I thought about how glad I was to be out of there and how many times I resisted the temptation to leave. And during this totally self-absorbed moment, God showed me something. As I was thinking about how miserable I was, God brought the thought of Jesus and His crucifixion to my mind. Actually, it was everything that led up to the crucifixion after His arrest.

The questioning, the beatings, the struggle to walk up Calvary's hill. And God whispered something to me that I should have seen years ago.

God pointed out to me that what Jesus endured was much worse than a long, uninteresting meeting. And He endured it for much longer than I sat still that night.

As I understand it, at any point during those agonizing hours, He could have said "Enough." He could have called on angels to come minister to Him. He could have stopped the whole process any time.

But He didn't.

Every step He took was a choice. No one forced Him to stand before Pilate and His accusers. No force on earth made Him withstand the beatings. Jesus said just before His arrest "Do you think I cannot call on My Father and He will at once put at My disposal more than twelve legions of angels? But how then would the Scriptures be fulfilled that say it must happen in this way?" Matthew 26:53-54

The guards and soldiers weren't what made Him go on. It was His love for humanity. His love for *me*. His desire to do His Father's will and the knowledge that this was the only way to bring about redemption for us. This was the only way for *me* to be able to be with *Him* for eternity. To me, that is astounding. Jesus did what He did, He took ALL that horrific pain - FOR ME.

The human side of Jesus didn't want to endure this pain. Who would? He even asked the Father to keep it from happening, but only *if there were any other way*. But since there was no other way, He endured it all. First the physical torment, and then the spiritual torture of having God turn His face away and being separated, for the first time, from the Father.

The soldiers didn't force Him up that hill and the nails didn't hold Him to the cross.

His love for me did.

That is a love that goes waaayyy beyond sitting through a long meeting.

October 2

"It is of the Lord's mercies that we are not consumed, because His compassions fail not. They are new every morning: great is Thy faithfulness." **Lamentations 3:22-23 (KJV)**

Tonight is Family Night at our church. Once a month, a different missions group provides a meal for the whole church. We have a great time of food and fellowship. Tonight is the youth group's turn.

Since my oldest is a youth, I'm there to help.

Josh, our youth minister, is directing the proceedings...beef hot dogs go here, chicken hot dogs go here, chili goes here, etc., etc. He is very good with the youth. He's full of energy and I've

never seen him when he wasn't smiling. I figured
that he would say the blessing before the meal
tonight.

Josh's prayers always start with "Thank You for this
good day."

I like that.

But today is October 2.

There have been numerous October 2nds that were
just run of the mill, average, every day days. And
there have been a couple of very good ones. My
good friends Mike and Dana got married that day.
It's my friend Cindy's birthday.

BUT, October 2 has also been a challenging day for
me in the past.

It has become my own personal "Ides of March."

October 2 is the day my son was diagnosed with the
same hereditary eye issue that I have. All his
appointments up until then had been clear...no sign
of the issue. But not on October 2. His diagnosis
meant surgery, patching, and a lifetime of glasses
and/or contacts to avoid the classification of legally
blind.

October 2 is the day my son and I moved out of our house when my first marriage finally collapsed.

And October 2 is the day my grandfather, Pa, died.

Unexpectedly.

He was not necessarily the picture of health, but no one expected it that day. He got up that morning, got on his riding lawn mower and rode up to where some men were working on the road. Came back in the house, sat down in his chair, and quit breathing.

I found out he had passed kind of by mistake. I had called my grandparents to see if I could come down that afternoon/night, take them to supper and spend the night with them - their house being only about 15 miles from where I was in college. My Daddy's cousin answered the phone...unusual, but not enough to make me think anything was wrong. Until she said "Are your parents there yet?" To which I replied "Why are my parents coming here?" I could hear her distress when she then said "Oh no...you don't know!"

So, for years I liked to pretend that October 2 didn't exist. Or say that I was going to spend the day wrapped in a bubble, sitting on my bed so I could make sure nothing bad happened.

But, obviously, that can't be done.

So, even though nothing bad happened today, and honestly, generally doesn't, I was preparing myself to hear Josh thank God for this "good day" when good is not a term I generally apply to October 2.

Josh didn't offer the prayer tonight. But I began to think about my past experiences with October 2 and applying Josh's "good day" attitude to those days.

The Bible says in Romans 8:28 "And we know that all things work together for good to them that love God, to them who are called according to His purpose."

I believe that. But I also believe that sometimes it takes the passage of time for us to be able to see how that can be accomplished. I also think that sometimes we won't know how God can work things "for good" this side of heaven. But we are assured that He can and does.

Looking back from the vantage point of many years removed, I can see how some things have worked for good. I didn't want Jackson, or any of my children, to deal with the vision issues I have dealt with, but they all do. The good part of all of this is that medical technology is better today than it was

35+ years ago. My surgeries were three- and four-day hospital stays. Theirs are outpatient. Their corrected eyesight is much better than mine is now and *far* better than it would have been had we done nothing.

I didn't want my first marriage to fall apart, but it did. I learned from that experience. I learned some things about myself and about other people. I saw the faithfulness and love of friends and family who supported me through that trying time. And God has chosen to bless me a few years later with a loving husband, two more children, and a happy home.

And my Pa? He is in heaven, pain free. I know that one day I will see him again. And hopefully we can play Concentration, Checkers, Hearts, Rummy or any other of the games we played together when I was a child.

An interim preacher at our church once said "Every day is a good day; some are just better than others." The verses from Lamentations tell us that we are not consumed because of God's mercies. To me that means that even as hard as things get, God's mercies are enough to carry me through. I may have to go day to day, but each day He will provide enough for me to carry on. He does not run out of mercy and His mercies are new every day.

Every day.

Even on October 2.

Car Seat Christianity

"So if the Son sets you free, you are truly free."
John 8:36 (NLT)

A few weeks ago, my girls and I had an extended period of "Girl Time." My son's 8th grade field trip to Washington, D.C. happened to coincide with my husband's annual Man Trip to the Mountains. So, for a few days we were without either one of them.

Wednesday night was GA (Girls In Action) night at church for my older daughter. She was ready to go even before we got home from school. She talked about it all day and asked about every 15 minutes "How much longer until we can go?"

I was already addled when it was time to leave. It had been one of those days that I felt like I was a step slow and not on my A game. I'm not even sure I was on my B game that day.

When it was finally time to go, I loaded her in the car and put her sister, now a toddler, in the car seat. Down the driveway we went, only to get halfway down and think to myself "Did I lock the door?"

So, back up the driveway we came so I could double check the door.

After checking the door (I had locked it), back in the car I went. And back down the driveway we went.

This time I made it a little further down the driveway before it dawned on me that I had not fastened Little Bit into her car seat.

I stopped the car, got out and walked around to her side of the car. When I opened the door, there she sat in the seat, in same position she was in when I set her in it a few minutes earlier.

She had not moved.

I don't think she realized that she wasn't strapped in and had all the freedom she needed to move around the car.

I'm glad she didn't. If she had, she probably would have made it into my lap.

After getting Elizabeth to GAs and heading to the nursery with Little Bit I thought about seeing my little one sitting there in her car seat.

She had all the freedom in the world to move, but hadn't even tried. I'm guessing because usually when she is in her car seat, she is strapped in and can't get up and move around.

How like that I am sometimes.

Sometimes I still think I act as if I haven't been set free. As if I am still bound by the unseen bonds that sin can have over us. I'm afraid to act because I might fail. Or I might not be good enough. Or I might not know what to say in a situation. Or because in the past I didn't handle a situation correctly. Or because somebody might have seen me acting in a "non-Christian way" and call me a hypocrite.

So, I just sit and do nothing.

Just like my Little Bit.

I, like her that night in her seat, don't fully realize the freedom I have been given in Christ. The gospel of John tells me that "So if the Son sets you free, you are truly free." I have no need to worry or fear because the Son has set me free. He has taken the penalty of sins away from me. He has removed them - ALL of them. He did it when He took my place on Calvary. And He sealed the deal when He rose on Easter morning, putting death in its place.

I am free.

Indeed.

I think the Chris Tomlinson song "My Chains are Gone/Amazing Grace" sums it up way better than I can. He sings:

My chains are gone
I've been set free
My God, my Savior has ransomed me
And like a flood His mercy reigns
Unending love, amazing grace

The Lord has promised good to me
His word my hope secures

He will my shield and portion be
As long as life endures

My God, My Savior *has ransomed me.*

Amen.

Spiritual Firewalls

"For in the day of trouble He will keep me safe in His dwelling; He will hide me in the shelter of His sacred tent and set me high upon a rock."
Psalm 27:5 (NIV)

Our Sunday School lesson began this morning with our teacher telling a story about his mother-in-law's laptop. She thought she had a virus on it so he was checking it for her. After examining it, he found she didn't have a virus on it but he did find evidence of 86,000 plus viral and/or cyber-attacks. I am about as far removed from computer literate as humanly possible, but that seems like a lot of cyber-attacks.

I have a virus blocker in my email and from time to time it quarantines something. I am advised in an email from my ISP not to open the quarantined email. I'm sure the cyber security on our home computers catches stuff we aren't aware of.

A few years ago, after hearing about the unexpected death of a young man we know, my husband and I looked him up on social media. In the process of "click here, click there" we found many things that made me sad. Posts full of expletives, disparaging remarks about groups of people, crude and vulgar comments.

To say I was appalled would be an understatement. I remember saying to my husband "There is a whole other world out there that I know nothing about." The pictures, the posts, the comments...those who posted those comments seemed so devoid of anything good. So empty...so hopeless...so sad. And so lost.

Because what you grow up with greatly influences your sense of what is normal, the things we saw seem so far away from normal to me. There was no place for vulgarity in my house as a child. I can only imagine what my Momma and Daddy would have done to me had I exhibited any of the behavior and/or language that was proudly displayed on social media.

Fear of the punishment that would have been doled out was a powerful incentive to keep me in check as a teenager. But at the same time, none of my friends were involved in things they shouldn't have been either.

Not that we were perfect by any stretch of the imagination, but there were lines that weren't crossed. I am sure that the prayers of my parents and grandparents made a difference. I pray for my children and their friends, too. I pray that they will choose friends who will be good influences on them. I pray that if someone tries to lead them down a path where they should not go, that they will be so uncomfortable that they can't stand it and won't go.

I wonder how many times, like the computer software, bad things are blocked from our lives unbeknownst to us. How often has God shielded us from something of which we were totally unaware? How often has He watched out for us when we didn't even know we were in danger? Scripture is full of references to God being our place of refuge and our shelter.

My guess is that if we could see our "spiritual firewall blocker tally sheet" we would be amazed at how much is kept from us.

Like the emails from my ISP that warn me of the dangers of opening questionable emails, God has given us warnings of things to stay away from in His Word.

One of my prayers is for God to extend, and expand, that protection on my family, friends, and most of all on my children and their friends. The world they are growing up in is vastly different from the one I grew up in. Not their homelife or the values they are being taught, but the world as a whole. Up is down, down is up, in is out and things that were once frowned upon are openly accepted, embraced and in some cases encouraged.

Change is not always good.

But one thing that is certain...God does not change. His Holiness has not changed. His expectations have not changed. His definition of right and wrong have not changed.

His love has not changed. His offer of forgiveness and extension of mercy are unchanged.

And the path to Him has not changed.

I pray that my son and older daughter will continue to grow in their relationship with Christ. I pray that my younger daughter will come to know Him at an early age. I pray that God will pull them to Him throughout their lives. And I pray that when they find themselves in sin, which at some point we all do, they will be made aware of it, repent and turn back to Him.

And I do pray for the hedge of protection (Job 1:10) to be **high, long, strong and thick**.

There can be no better, safer place of refuge than in Him.

I Read This Book Once

"All Scripture is inspired by God and is useful to teach us what is true and to make us realize what is wrong in our lives. It corrects us when we are wrong and teaches us to do what is right."
II Timothy 3:16 (NLT)

I subscribe to a couple of daily devotions. Usually I try to read them while eating breakfast before the kids get up. One morning as I glanced at my email the title of the Girlfriends in God devotion (this one by Gwen Smith) caught my eye. It was titled "What Every Woman Needs to Know..." but I couldn't read the rest of the subject line because I was looking at it on my phone.

I thought for a split second it was going to say "What Every Woman Needs to Know About Men." That would have been funny.

My husband and I have a running joke about knowing all there is to know about the opposite sex. It stems from a female friend saying to him years ago "I read this book. Now I know how *all* men are." (I have no idea what the book was and I'm sure he doesn't either.)

The absurdity of this blanket statement stayed with him and we joke about it from time to time. Sometimes one of us will say to the other when generalizing about something, "See...I read this book once."

Saying that a book can tell how all one group of people are seems silly to me. While I do think there are certain things that men are more drawn to in general, and while there are similarities among many of the men I know, to say that they are all the same is ludicrous. Even among the men who are most important in my life there are vast differences.

My husband, dad, brother, uncles, cousins, and friends are all unique and have their own distinct personalities.

My Daddy is a talker. He is gifted at being able to know what to say and can make conversation with almost anyone. I often wish I had his gift for being able to do that. My husband is quieter, an avid reader and probably the most intelligent person I have ever met. My brother and brother-in-law are two of the hardest working people I know. My uncles and cousins are unique in their own regard and gifted in different ways.

So, her comment about knowing how "all men" are strikes me as totally unrealistic.

But the title of the devotion, paired with my brain's jump to our little joke, got me thinking.

There is a Book that I can read that will give me insight into every aspect of life.

The Bible.

It is full of wisdom.

Advice.

Miracles.

Hope.

All the books in the Bible are different just like all the men who are part of my life are different, but there isn't one that I can't learn something from. While some are easier to read and understand than others, each book has something in it for me.

Some speak loudly, some whisper truth, some step on my toes. Sometimes I can read a passage that I have read countless times before and it speaks to me in a new way.

That is what is so amazing to me. The Bible, written so many years ago, by so many different people, can speak in so many ways to each of us, today.

I try to read my Bible every morning. Some mornings, I miss. I can tell a difference in my overall attitude when I miss.

Even though my bookshelves are crowded to the point of overflowing, there are only a few books that I have read more than once. Few that I feel like I have the time to reread.

The Bible should be an exception. I should be able to say every day, "See...I read this Book."

Surely Lord You Don't Mean Me

"Do everything without grumbling or arguing, so that you may become blameless and pure, 'children of God without fault in a warped and crooked generation.' Then you will shine among them like stars in the sky."
Philippians 2:14 (NIV)

"Ants got into the banana bread."

Not exactly what I had been expecting to hear from my husband when I got home. It got worse.

"And in the oven, too."

I will admit that as far as housekeepers go, I'm not the best. In fact, I'd say that being a good housekeeper is not a talent I possess. But this shocked even me.

The day before, our daughter and I had made a loaf of banana bread. It was delicious! And it actually turned out looking good. Preparing pretty food is another skill I do not possess. But this loaf had it all...great taste and good form.

But now it was ruined.

I'm not sure how the ants got into the oven, but somehow, they had found the loaf. And made it their own.

So, out to the dog the loaf went, into the sink the pan went, and to work I went. Cleaning the oven.

Not a happy camper.

And grumbling to myself as I went. This was not how I had planned to spend the few moments between coming home from doing things with the kids and taking our son to his guitar lesson.

So, I scrubbed. And I thought pitiful thoughts. Poor me. Pitiful me. Scrubbing this nasty oven. Aggravating ants. Messed up my bread.

Then I heard a small, small voice in my mind. "Do all things without grumbling and complaining."

This verse is one that we have pointed out to our son on quite a few occasions when he has been less than thrilled to do something he needed to do. But surely it doesn't apply to me while cleaning a messy oven!

But it does.

As I stood there, many of the blessings I have came to mind.

I had been to the library with my mom, my kids, my sister-in-law and my two young nieces.

How many people would love to have a family that they enjoy doing things with?

How many people would love to live close enough to their families to be able to do things like that?

How many people would like to have the free time during the week to be able to do what I had just done?

And why is my oven messy? (Apart from the fact that I hadn't cleaned it in a while.)

Because I cook food in it. Often. There is always food in my refrigerator, my freezer, and in my cabinets. When I run out of something I need, I go to the store. There is enough in my checking account to get what I need at the grocery store.

As I stood there thinking about it, I realized that my attitude wasn't so great. I had a mess to clean up, yes, and I didn't enjoy it, but I am blessed. So very, very blessed. My attitude should be one of thanksgiving, so that I can "shine among them like stars in the sky."

Even when my oven is less than shiny.

The "Rightness" in Wrong Words

"For a Child is born to us, a Son is given to us. The government will rest on His shoulders. And He will be called: Wonderful Counselor, Mighty God, Everlasting Father, Prince of Peace."
Isaiah 9:6 (NLT)

While driving home tonight from my son's cross country meet my daughter was singing Vacation Bible School songs at high volume from the back seat.

Yes to the blessings
Of studying God's Word
Yes to the best thing
Jesus is More!

We've been listening to these songs for *months* now.

That's not how that song goes, I thought to myself. It's "Jesus is Lord," not "Jesus is More!"

That particular song is one that once it has begun to play in my head, I can't stop hearing it. Now I was hearing it with the wrong words.

Or was I?

Maybe Elizabeth, in her 3-year-old way, was on to something.

Jesus is more than a good man. There is no doubt that Jesus was a good man. He met people's needs, was kind, and spent time with the oppressed and the people no one else wanted to be around. He brought hope to the hopeless. There have been many good men in the world, but good men can't do all that He did. He is more.

Jesus is a good teacher. He used easy parables, stories, and illustrations to help people understand the things He talked about. He knew His audience (really knew His audience!) and spoke in ways that they could understand. He was patient with people, teaching concepts again and again. But good teachers can't do all that He did. He is more.

Jesus is so much more.

Isaiah gives us a list, which is by no means comprehensive of ways that Christ Jesus can be described.

He *is* the Wonderful Counselor.

He *is* the Mighty God.

He *is* the Everlasting Father.

He *is* the Prince of Peace.

Each of these assurances alone is impressive. But Isaiah doesn't say that Jesus is one and not the other, or three out of four. He is ALL of these. At the same time. All at once.

I sometimes have a hard time being one thing well. Jesus is all of these, and more.

He is the Great I AM.

Jesus is more. And more. And more. Like my Elizabeth sang, Jesus is more. And Jesus is more than enough.

Putting Mommy to Shame

Once again, my older daughter has put me to shame. Twice in just a few days regarding the same situation.

This past Saturday she had her second basketball game of the season. She had a great time running around, playing, and learning basketball basics. The 8:30 a.m. games last a little longer than an hour, including the halftime. So by the time it is over, everyone is hungry.

After this game we decided to get some breakfast. The grandparents went with us. The little restaurant we went to is on main street, which means parking is sometimes not the easiest to find. My husband, our younger daughter, and I parked at the end of the street before walking up to meet our star player and her grandparents who had found parking near the back of the restaurant.

We then did some major damage to our New Year's resolutions to eat healthier!

When we finished, we all walked toward our car.

Gathered at the courthouse and on either side of the main street were three groups of people. They were protesting. Exactly what they were protesting I'm not sure. Recently our little town experienced some ugly divisiveness over a statue that has been standing at the courthouse for a long, long time. Every Saturday for months there have been people opposed to the statue, and those in favor of keeping it where it was, holding signs, chanting and occasionally hollering at each other.

The statue came down in the middle of the night several weeks ago.

I thought things would quiet down.

And as a whole I guess they have.

But this past Saturday, people were out again.

We had to walk by them to get to our car. The loudest and biggest group was on the opposite side of the street from our car. They were having a shouting match against no one in particular as far as I could tell. Shout. Chant. Whoop. Holler.

The rallying cry they had taken up as we neared them was "God doesn't exist! God doesn't exist! God doesn't exist!" Then they would holler, apparently very proud of themselves for their cleverness and start the chant all over.

I'm glad we live in a country where people are free to gather and chant their beliefs. But that is where my agreement of what they were doing stops.

My older daughter stopped and watched.

And listened.

When we got in the car, she asked about it. Her Daddy and I explained as well as we could that different people have different beliefs and that not everyone she will come in contact with believes in God and Jesus.

To say that she has thought about it is an understatement.

It has eaten her up.

She has talked about it and talked about it. And asked repeatedly "How can anyone think God isn't real?"

Every day since then.

But the kicker to it all is what she has said about them. She told me "Momma. That's sad. We should pray for them."

I am so proud of her for saying that, especially because my initial thought was not that we should pray for them. My thought was "I wish they would be quiet and just go away." Isn't that a kind and Christian attitude to have?

But we *should* pray for them.

And so she has.

Every day since then.

Every time we have had our family prayer time she has mentioned "those people who don't believe in You."

I haven't remembered to pray for them. But she has.

The other thing that put me to shame is the way she prayed for them the other night. She had just said "Be with those people who don't believe in You." And then she followed that with something along the lines of "God, send Your angels to help show them and help them believe in You."

I was amazed.

Not because she was praying for them again, but the "bigness" of her prayer.

I had not thought about asking God to send His angels. But she did. God only sends His angels for big things, right? Like announcing the birth of the Savior, or announcing the birth of John the Baptist.

But in reality, this is a big deal. The souls, *the eternal destination*, of these people are at stake. My daughter asked Him to move in a supernatural way to bring these people into a right relationship with Him. She didn't merely ask for them to start believing or for other people to help, but for God to send His heavenly servants down to earth to work a miracle.

She did so boldly. Just like the scripture from Hebrews 4 says. She asked in her confident way of prayer. And again I saw the evidence of her faith in her all-knowing, all-powerful and Almighty God.

I'm quite sure she doesn't realize how the faith of a child can demonstrate true faith.

But I'm glad it does.

Changing My Tune

"And we are confident He hears us whenever we ask for anything that pleases Him."
I John 5:14 (NLT)

Over the past few days my middle child has begun to ask to listen to certain songs on my phone's YouTube app. She, like many 6-year-olds, gets locked in on one or two particular things - in this case a song - and that is the one she wants to hear. Over and over again.

Mercifully, I like the two she has been hooked on this past week.

The one that she has chosen to listen to the most is Michael W. Smith's live version of "Mighty to Save."

She loves it. We have listened to it over and over again in the car and in the house. She sings along with the recording.

It is a great song. But after hearing it multiple times on multiple days, it does get a little old.

My oldest, who is often in the car with us, has reached his point of total saturation.

This morning on the way to school, she asked if she could listen to "Mighty to Save" again. I asked Jackson to pull it up for her and as he was unlocking my phone, he said "Elizabeth, why don't you listen to a different song?"

Her immediate response was "Yes! I want to hear…" and then she named a song that shall remain nameless here. It was nothing I had ever heard of because it was recorded after I quit listening to new music, which happened sometime around 1993.

In fact, it is a new song. Jackson groaned and said "That's even worse!"

I laughed and said "Be careful what you wish for son!"

Elizabeth did as he asked her to do. She requested something different. But unbeknownst to him, it was not a change for the better.

After listening to the song she chose, I agreed with Jackson. It was *not* a change for the better.

I thought about that on the way home from school.

I am sure, on countless occasions, I have said to God, "Come on! It's time for something different!" Or "No, let me go this way." And I am sure that the times He has answered "no" have been because He knows that what I think I need isn't what I need at all. That the direction I want to go would be bad. Worse than the situation I find myself in already.

There have been prayers God didn't answer in the way in which I wanted. I didn't know it at the time, but in retrospect, I can see how His answer was far better than what I was praying for. I need to be careful what I pray for and how I pray.

I think that is why it is so important for us to pray that our desires line up with God's will. **He** knows what is best for me. **I** don't.

He is all knowing. I am not.

The things that He has planned for us are better than the things we could imagine for ourselves. Jeremiah 29:11 assures us of that. "For *I* know the plans *I* have for you, declares the Lord" (emphasis mine). Nowhere does it even hint at "For Suzanne knows the plans..."

When my children ask me for something that would not be good for them, I say "No." Not because I don't want them to be happy. But because I love them. I'm more concerned with their long-term welfare, safety, character development, you name it, than their immediate gratification. They often don't understand that. I don't expect them to understand. But I do expect that they trust that I have their best interest in mind and would never intentionally steer them wrong.

Same with me. I don't always know. But God does. Knowing that I should temper my requests with praying that *His* will be done, and more specifically that His will becomes what I want. That I can accept that His answer is always right, always perfect and always on time.

And, like I told my oldest, "Be careful what you wish for!"

Daughter

"And He said to her, 'Daughter your faith has made you well. Go in peace. You have been healed.'"
Mark 5:34 (NLT)

I imagine this scene in Mark to be chaotic. Big crowds, lots of noise, lots of people. Everyone vying for Christ's attention.

In the crowd is a woman who has been miserable for 12 years. Physically uncomfortable, socially outcast, and emotionally out of steam. One simple act on her part changes all of that. And shed light on something for me this morning.

This is a story I have read many times. It is one of my favorite examples of Christ's mercy in the Bible.

Up until this morning, the focus for me has always
been on the word "daughter" - I even have it
underlined in my Bible. I connect with that word. I
am one...I have two. I'm proud to be my Momma
and Daddy's daughter. In fact, often upon meeting
someone new, if they are from the same place I am
from, I tell them whose child I am.

I also tell people whose Momma I am. And I hope,
one day, my children will be proud to tell others
whose (and Whose) child they are.

So "daughter" in this verse has always spoken to
me. I like to imagine Christ calling me
"daughter"...claiming me as His own, speaking in
that one word all the love that comes from a parent
to a child, all the security, all the comfort that
comes from just being with your parent.

But today what caught my attention was a few
words after: "Go in peace." I am a worrier by
nature. If there isn't something going on in my little
world for me to worry about, I will create it in my
mind. And worry. And worry. And worry.

I'm sure this woman worried too. Worried about her
physical condition, worried about being ostracized
by society, worried about how she was going to
keep going after ineffective treatments. But on this

day, we see that she had done all she needed to do. She, in faith, reached out and touched the hem of His cloak. When He spoke to her, what did He tell her?

"Go in peace."

And who was the Man who told her to "go in peace?" **The Prince of Peace Himself!**

Isn't that what He is saying to me…"Suzanne, go in Peace. You've trusted Me with your eternal life, don't you think I can handle your earthly life? I *have* taken care of things…I *am* taking care of things. I *will* take care of things. Let go. Don't worry!"

I don't think Jesus wants us to go blindly through life, not having a single care in the world. I do believe He expects us to be prepared and to be wise, but I, for sure, could take a lesson from the lady here in Scripture.

When the worry sets in, reach out to Him, spend a moment with Him (spend a moment more with Him), and then "Go in peace."

I Was Blind

"He replied, 'Whether He is a sinner or not, I don't know. One thing I do know. I was blind but now I see!'"
John 9:25 (NIV)

Anyone who has ever spent much time around small children knows how many questions they can come up with.

And how often they can ask the same one.

Sometimes, how quickly they can ask the same question repeatedly.

"Mommy, where is my Ted?"

"Momma, where are my shoes?"

"Momma, why won't this app download to the computer?"

"Mommy!!! Where is Brudder?"

These questions I can usually handle (except the one about the app). Then there are others that I don't handle as well.

Usually those are the ones that aren't from my children, but ones I ask myself.

"Why did I do *that*?"

"Why do my kids have to have this eye problem?"

"Where did I put my glasses/car keys/coffee cup?"

"Why didn't God answer that prayer the way *I* wanted Him to?"

In this story from the Gospel of John is a man who is asked questions over and over again by people who should have known the answer. Jesus had healed him. A whole new world had opened up for him, in more than one way, and he was being grilled by the Jewish religious leaders.

He answers them. They badger him. He answers them. They badger him some more. They badger his parents.

I love his final answer to them.

Cuts right to the chase.

The man answered, "Whether He is a sinner or not, I don't know. One thing I do know. I was blind but now I see!"

I think oftentimes we get too hung up on the things we don't have the ability to answer. The things that we may not ever understand this side of heaven. When really we ought to do as this man did, focus on the One who does the healing, the One who does know and what we have experienced through Him.

If I were to apply this thought more often I would be a much better witness. I wouldn't worry about what to say when a non-believer asked me a question I don't know the answer to. I could simply say what this blind man did. "I don't know, but what I do know is this..." and talk about what He has done for me in my life.

I don't understand why some prayers aren't answered the way I wanted. But I can tell you about countless ones that were answered in ways I could not have imagined.

I don't understand why bad things happen. But I do know Who has carried me through the dark times of my life when bad things happened to me.

I don't fully understand *how*, but I know that my sins *are* forgiven.

And I know that the love of the One who forgave me is where I need to focus my mind.

But now I see!

Inferno Dragons

"For the message of the cross is foolishness to those who are perishing, but to us who are being saved, it is the power of God."
I Corinthians 1:18 (NIV)

A month or so ago, I volunteered to drive for a bowling trip my son's class was going on. My car is not huge, but without Little Bit's car seat I could transport my son and a couple of other kids.

So, Jackson and two classmates rode with me.

There was much conversation, laughter and even a little debate going on as we made our way to the bowling alley.

But I didn't understand a word of what they were saying to each other.

I was listening, but I am pretty sure they were speaking in a foreign language. Perhaps one of their own making, but it wasn't English as I know it.

I heard things about "inferno dragons" and "the nether" and "ghasts." Among other things.

When we got to the bowling alley I found other adults just to make sure I hadn't lost the ability to communicate.

I had forgotten about it for the most part until two nights ago.

One of Jackson's friends came over to spend the night with us. During supper, there was again a form of communication I am not familiar with taking place. I will call it "teenageboyese." It consisted of phrases that made no sense, laughter, a random assortment of normal words, more laughter, the occasional snort, even more laughter, and an odd collection of non-human sounds.

Generally followed by more laughter.

The boys seemed to understand each other perfectly.

I exchanged glances a couple of times with my husband just to make sure I wasn't missing anything. To my relief, he looked just as befuddled at their exchanges as I was.

I'm sure that there were times in the 80's and early 90's when my parents looked at me the same way I looked at the boys the other night, convinced that they brought the wrong baby home from the hospital. My generation had our way of saying things and using phrases that our parents didn't use.

Just like every generation has.

As I thought about their exchanges and my total lack of comprehension, I began to think about how we as church going Christians need to watch how we speak when we talk with non-believers. I don't necessarily mean I need to make sure I don't let any four-letter words slip out (although I think that would be proper). What I mean is the use of churchy sounding words that others may not understand.

I am not the best at witnessing to people.

But when I do, I don't need to try to sound like I'm working on my Ph.D. in theology with a concentration in semantics. (Quite sure I wouldn't be convincing in that regard anyway.) Just honest talk about my God and what He has done in my life.

The Bible clearly tells us in I Corinthians that the message of the cross is totally different to those of us who have a relationship with Christ than those who don't. My main objective ought to be to share what God means to me and share the love of Jesus. Share what He has done for me and the hope that He offers to everyone.

Keeping it simple keeps people from needing a translator.

Like I needed with those teenage boys.

Reminders in the Sky

"The Lord bless you and keep you. The Lord make His face shine on you and be gracious to you; the Lord turn His face towards you and give you peace." **Numbers 6:24-27 (NLT)**

It was a gray, rainy, yucky day.

And it mirrored my mood.

It was one of those days when nothing really terrible happened...just a string of annoyances. The sum total of these had me into a really foul mood.

After spending most of the late morning and afternoon playing phone tag with the pediatrician's office and various pharmacies, I was finally able to

get a different prescription called in for my daughter
for a condition I thought was cured.

The fact that we were dealing with it again had me
flustered and aggravated.

Grrrrr.

After picking up our son at school, he and I went to
town to get the medicine the doctor had called in for
my daughter while she stayed home with Daddy.
My son was less than thrilled about having to go to
town, but that at least usually means an order of
fries for him.

We parked in front of the pharmacy and went in.
Just after I stepped into the door, the phone rang.
It was the pharmacy with the automated message
"There has been a delay in your prescription."

Grrrrr.

I went on back to the pharmacy hoping that it was
just an issue with insurance. Even though just an
issue with insurance is a frustration in and of itself.

However, once getting to the pharmacy, the clerk
told me that they were out of the medicine. The
soonest they could get it was the next day. Not

good enough when your child is in need. The pharmacy employee was very helpful and called the same pharmacy in a neighboring town. They had it and assured me that they would hold it for me.

So, back to the car, in the rain, to head 20 miles up the road to the next town.

This did not help my mood.

Grrrrr again.

Once arriving in the next town we headed straight to the pharmacy. Although they had it, I was still in no better of a mood.

I had told my son we would get his french fries, so the next stop was the fast-food restaurant. We pulled into the drive through line, but it was anything but "fast" food. Both lanes were open but we sat for a good 15 minutes.

And, after we pulled off, we realized the order was wrong.

Grrrrr Grrrrr Grrrrr.

Before leaving town I decided it would be wise to fill up the car.

So I pulled in the gas station. Parked and stepped out.

Right into a mud puddle.

Grrrrr Grrrrr Grrrrr Grrrrr.

After shoving the hose into my gas tank, I turned around and saw it.

A beautiful rainbow in the otherwise gray sky.

And something in my mood changed.

I stood there for a second, thinking about the message in the sky. The reminder of God's promise to Noah thousands of years ago. A promise never to destroy the earth again through a flood.

It wasn't that I felt like the world was about to be destroyed, or that my life was being destroyed by the events of the day, but I had let them destroy my joy in the day.

And that wasn't good.

Standing there with wet feet, I thought back on the day and my reaction to things. There had been no "big bad things," just some small aggravating ones. I had been so focused on the negatives, the things that hadn't gone the way I wanted, that I hadn't paid attention to the blessings.

For one, we have a wonderful pediatrician's office. They spent a great deal of time on the phone with me trying to help me determine the best course of action for my little one.

We live where there is medicine that I can get to help her.

We were - ultimately - able to get the medicine. And given that we had met our deductible multiple times over this year, there was no additional charge.

Even though the fast-food order wasn't 100% correct, we were able to get my son some french fries and me a warm cup of coffee. A nice treat on a rainy day.

The rain was helping with the mild drought we are having.

I had a few minutes alone with my son who is growing up way too fast. Just the two of us, which gave us a chance to talk and catch up. Something we don't always get to do.

The rainbow was just the little nudge from above that I needed to readjust my attitude. A reminder not to get so bent out of shape over the small, ultimately insignificant things that I had allowed to consume me.

My choir director from high school, the late, great Polly Yow always ended the church services at which we sang with the same benediction, "The Lord Bless You and Keep You," taken from Numbers 6. She invited any former choir members to come to the front of the church and join in singing the benediction. It was always something special for current and former students to join together in singing these words.

It felt to me that the rainbow was the Lord reminding me of those words (which will always be set to music in my mind!), turning His face towards me and reminding me about all that *is right* with my life. All the blessings that I have. All the reasons I have to be grateful and thankful to Him. All the blessings He has bestowed on me throughout my life.

Even on a gray rainy day.

Joy to the World

"And the angel said unto them, 'Fear not: for, behold, I bring you good tidings of great Joy which shall be to all people. For unto you is born this day in the City of David, a Saviour which is Christ the Lord.'"

Luke 2:10-12 (KJV)

This morning on the way to school my daughter asked if we could turn the CD player on and listen to a song. She wanted to listen to the "Game On" CD from Vacation Bible School from a year or two ago.

When I turned my CD player on, a different disc started playing. When my daughter recognized it, she changed her mind and wanted to listen to it. Specifically to song number 3.

My son looked at me as if to ask me "Are you really going to let her listen to that?"

Not because of any questionable lyrics or anything.

But because the CD in question is "Peace on Earth" by Casting Crowns.

It's a Christmas CD. And the song she wanted to hear is "Joy to World."

And today is May 1. It's just a few weeks after Easter.

Not usually when one listens to Christmas music. But we did. And it was great!

The more I thought about it, the more I thought that even though "Joy to the World" is typically only sung in December, there is no reason it can't fit in to the Easter season as well.

Think about the lyrics to "Joy to the World" and how they can also apply to Easter.

"Joy to the World - the Lord is come! Let Earth receive her King." Christ came as a baby at Christmas and then came back from the dead at

Easter. For us. Proof that He is indeed King over all. He is Lord over all. We should rejoice and receive Him.

"Let every heart, prepare Him room." Shouldn't we prepare our heart for Him. Look at what He has done for us. Our hearts should be open and ready to receive Him.

"And heaven and nature sing! And Heaven and nature sing! And Heaven and Heaven and nature sing!" In another passage of Scripture Jesus tells the Jewish leaders that if He asked His followers to be quiet as He rode into Jerusalem, then the stones themselves would shout out. I think the beauty of nature during Spring is a way that nature does in fact "sing" and cry out, showing His majesty.

It didn't occur to my daughter that "Joy to the World" is a Christmas song. I, initially, didn't really want to listen to a Christmas song in May. But it really does fit Easter, too.

Listening to the Christmas music right after the Easter season kind of wrapped up the whole story. Easter couldn't have happened without Christmas, and Christmas is meaningless without Easter. Santa is nice and the Easter Bunny is fun, but the birth of Christ and His death and resurrection are the true meaning of the seasons. And truly they go hand in hand.

Joy to the World!

The Lord is come.

He Healed Them All

"News about Him spread as far as Syria, and people soon began bringing to Him all who were sick. And whatever their sickness or disease, or if they were demon possessed or epileptic or paralyzed—He healed them all."
Matthew 4:24 (NLT)

Sometimes when reading through my Bible, things that are pretty basic to the Christian faith stand out and I see something I haven't seen before.

And they stick with me.

That happened when reading this passage the other day. This time the truth was about Jesus's healing power.

The news about Jesus had begun to spread in the ancient world. Of course since Verizon hadn't come on the scene yet there were no text messages from friend to friend saying "Hey, you gotta come see this guy!" or anything like that. News spread by actual word of mouth.

This verse tells us that the news of Him had spread as far as Syria. I'm *really* bad at geography so I had to look this up, but that is a pretty good distance from Israel when the fastest form of transportation was by camel.

The news of Jesus's healing powers was to be sure welcome news to the sick and to those who cared for and about them. Anyone who has ever cared for someone who is sick knows how difficult and frustrating it can be when you've done all that you can for them and they are still sick.

Jesus offered hope to the physically sick.

He also offered hope to the spiritually sick.

The very last few words of this verse are so comforting. "He healed them all."

It doesn't say "He healed the ones with insurance."

It doesn't say "He healed the ones who were related to the powerful."

It doesn't say "He healed the ones who could afford to give Him a good meal afterwards."

It doesn't say "He healed the young and handsome."

It says "He healed them all."

I like to read it this way: "He. Healed. Them. ALL."

Jesus had compassion on those in need, and He could do something about it.

So He did.

This particular verse lists only a few of the ailments that Jesus healed: epilepsy, paralysis, demon possession. But from other scriptures we know that He healed numerous other ailments, even raising the dead!

And the best news of all? Jesus *still* heals. And He can heal "them ALL." And even more comforting? "Them" is us.

Jesus can take the broken marriage and restore it.

Jesus can take the addict and release the addiction.

Jesus can take the depressed and give them hope.

Jesus can give the strength needed to offer forgiveness to others.

Jesus has been called the Great Physician. It is nice to know that there isn't a condition out there that He can't handle.

And you never have to wait for an appointment.

Last Minute Forgiveness

"Jesus answered him, 'Truly I tell you, today you will be with Me in paradise.'"
Luke 23:43 (NIV)

Never again will I miss getting my flu shot.

It started with a little tickle in my throat which is how all my head colds start. No reason to worry.

Then almost as suddenly as turning on the light, I was sick. And I do mean, sick. Body aches, high fever, a splitting headache, chills, the whole deal. A trip to the doctor as soon as I could get an appointment confirmed what I was pretty sure of already.

Flu.

This is the first year (and it will be the last) that I haven't gotten the shot.

Now, after two doses of the antiviral, I can at least be on the couch. I've read some and been on the Internet some.

It is amazing what you can find online.

While doing some reading online, I came across an book with an interesting title: <u>My Grandfather Would Have Shot Me</u>. As someone who had, in my opinion, two of the best grandfathers ever, I found the title intriguing.

As it turns out, it is the story of a young black woman who finds out that her maternal grandfather was Amon Goth, the commandant of the Kraków-Płaszów concentration camp in Płaszów during the German-occupation of Poland during World War II. Her mother was his daughter, her father was from Nigeria.

Talk about shocking.

It is because of my grandfather that I was reading such articles. My Pa was the son of a Polish Jew who immigrated to the US in the late 1800s or early 1900s. I'm not sure of the date that my great-grandfather arrived at Ellis Island. (And wish I had checked with my Pa.) Pa was a history buff, and he passed that love on to me.

I thought about what a horrific realization it must have been for this young lady to learn that her grandfather was responsible for the deaths of many, many people. To learn that her grandfather personally shot upwards of 30 people (depending on the source you research), that she was related to "Hitler's Butcher." And to top that horror off, to realize what he probably would have thought of her, simply because of her skin color.

As a human being, I think of him as a monster.

As the descendant of Polish Jews, I wonder if any of my relatives were subjected to Goth's atrocities. I wonder why my great-grandfather's family left Poland when they did. What if they had stayed? Would I even be here?

I wonder if Goth had any remorse for his behavior. I wonder, if, at the end of his life, he knew it was wrong. I wonder.

Goth was tried for his war atrocities and executed in Poland in 1946.

In my opinion, he got what he deserved.

Death.

To be on planet Earth no more. To be where he cannot inflict pain on anyone ever again. Dead. Dead. Dead.

But, in death, his soul is somewhere.

As I thought about this last night, it occurred to me that as horrible as I think he was, God could have forgiven him. Even if it was moments before his death, the God of unimaginable mercy would have forgiven him, if Goth sincerely asked in repentance and accepted Christ as the only way to heaven.

I find it hard to fathom that atrocities of that nature can be forgiven.

But Christ shows just such "last minute mercy" on Golgotha. Luke tells us that on each side of Jesus a criminal was being executed. A criminal, a bad person by human standards. Yet even as they hung there, with death imminent, one asked for Christ's forgiveness.

And it was granted.

What that says to me is that not only is Christ capable of unimaginable mercy, but it is a reminder that His death was for *everyone*. His forgiveness is for *everyone,* for those people we consider good, and for those people we consider bad.

Even those I consider monstrous.

He Walked on Water

"He saw that they were in serious trouble, rowing hard and struggling against the wind and waves. About three o'clock in the morning Jesus came toward them, walking on the water. He intended to go past them, but when they saw Him walking on the water, they cried out in terror, thinking He was a ghost. They were all terrified when they saw Him. But Jesus spoke to them at once. 'Don't be afraid,' He said. 'Take courage! I am here!' Then He climbed into the boat, and the wind stopped." **Mark 6:48-51 (NLT)**

Randy Travis had a song years ago called "He Walked On Water." It was one of my favorites on that particular cassette tape (which really dates me). The song is about the special relationship between the singer and his great-grandfather. The chorus repeats "Cause I thought...he walked...on water." The point is to convey just how much the singer loves his great-grandfather. I know how he feels.

I didn't know any of my great-grandfathers, but I was blessed to know both of my granddaddies. I was fortunate enough to have Pa until I was a sophomore in college, and my Papa until I was 39. Blessed also that they lived close by and I got to spend a good amount of time with each of them. They were different from each other in some ways, alike in other ways.

Pa was a game player. We spent hours playing Checkers, Carrom, and Concentration (a regular deck of cards version of memory).

Papa wasn't as much into games, except maybe Rook, which we played on his side porch. Papa was a "peacemaker" as he liked to say, even as he would carry on with anyone he came in contact with.

I have found myself passing along things I did with them, and things they said, to my children. My kids know how to play Concentration. About a month ago as I was driving my son to his guitar lesson, it began to rain really hard. I found myself talking to my son about how to drive, something Papa did almost every time we were in the car together.

I thought Pa and Papa walked on water, just like the singer in the Randy Travis song. After the song went off the radio I decided to look up the passages of Scripture about the One who quite literally walked on water.

I like this translation from Mark best of all, especially two specific parts.

The first: "He saw that they were in serious trouble." I believe Jesus and God see all and know all. But here the Scripture explicitly states it. *He saw*. And because He saw (and had compassion for the disciples), He did something about it. He didn't just walk on by. He got in the boat. Got in the boat **with them.** Didn't fix it from a distance, although He certainly could have, He came closer. Directly to them. He became personally involved in their situation.

He can do the same for me. He sees me when I am struggling, or afraid, or confused. He knows my trials and He can do something about them.

The second part of this translation that I really like is what He said to the terrified disciples. "Don't be afraid. Take courage! I am here!" What really stands out to me here is the "take courage" part. "Take." Jesus is encouraging His followers to be brave. But the word used here, in this translation, is an active word. "Take." It involves actually *doing* something.

The image it creates for me is reaching out and grabbing something, the same way I might take something someone is handing me. Physically taking it. I interpret it as kinda "Reach out and be brave. Grab the reassurance. Grab the comfort of being with the One who can fix it." What is needed is there, we just have to reach out and take it. Jesus Himself is handing it to us.

My husband is fond of quoting a verse that his mother taught him when he was a young child: "What time I am afraid, I will trust in You." (Psalm 56:3) I **will** trust in You.

Reach out. Take what God has given me and trust. Start by looking to Him.

I once saw a sign that said "My Lifeguard walks on water."

Yes.

Yes, He does.

Always a Teacher

"I urge you, first of all, to pray for all people. Ask God to help them; intercede on their behalf, and give thanks for them."
I Timothy 2:1 (NLT)

Last weekend my girls and I went to a chicken tender benefit supper. This one was held at my niece's school, the same school her Daddy/my brother, my Mom, my Grandmother and I all attended. My niece is in kindergarten and wanted the whole family to come. The meal was a fundraiser to generate funds for the 8th grade at her school to put towards their Washington, D.C. field trip.

Only three of the five of us from my little family could go since the supper was the same weekend as Hubby's Man Trip to the Mountains and our son's 8th grade class field trip to Washington, D.C.

But she didn't have to ask me twice to come.

I love my little niece.

And I love fried chicken.

So my girls and I went. Clara, my niece, was excited to show us the cafeteria where she eats lunch every day and point out some of the other things at her school. It looks waaaayyyyy different than it did when I started kindergarten there in 1979.

It was a great time. We got to spend time with my parents, my brother, my sister-in-law and their three girls. AND the chicken was really good. I also got to see many people from home who I don't see very often anymore.

One person I saw was a former high school teacher. Had him for two classes...one my sophomore year and one my senior year. It's funny that I thought he was old when he was my teacher. He was probably younger then than I am now.

He and his wife sat down near the table where my family was sitting. We exchanged pleasantries and then it was on to the task at hand...eating some chicken tenders.

I wasn't trying to eavesdrop on them but I couldn't help overhearing the blessing he said over the meal. He prayed for the food and that it would be a blessing, he thanked God for the food and then he did something that really stood out to me.

He prayed for all the children at that school.

Not by name of course. It's a small country school, but there are still several hundred kids there. But he did ask the Almighty to bless each child who attended school there. Then he went a step further and asked that God would save each and every one. That each and every child would receive Jesus as his or her Savior.

It was beautiful.

And it made me see my former teacher in a whole new light.

I wonder how many of those children have someone who prays for them on a daily basis. There are some for sure. But there are bound to be some who don't. My teacher lifted them all before God. He demonstrated Paul's admonition to "pray for all people."

His prayer also covered the "help them" portion of Paul's instructions. What greater help could these children have than having Jesus as their Lord and Savior? What greater help could any of us have?

His prayer was so simple, yet so meaningful. It was a wonderful example of Biblical obedience. Christ died for all. We are instructed to pray for all. I am pretty good at remembering to pray for the people I am closest to...my family and friends, church members, etc. But this is an area I could really do better in.

Why not say a quick prayer for all the other people in the grocery store when I go in? (And as often as I go in, that would cover lots of people!)

Why not pray for the other parents sitting in the gym during the many basketball games our kids are a part of?

Why not pray for the other drivers that I'll meet on the road before I pull out of my driveway?

Nothing big, nothing fancy. Just something simple.
Just ask God to keep His hand on them. Bless
them. Protect them. Like my teacher did.

I don't remember specifically what I learned in
either of his classes because it has been almost 30
years since high school.

But I sure did learn from him at the chicken tender
dinner.

I Know You Hear Us

"And this is the confidence that we have toward Him, that if we ask anything according to His will He hears us. And if we know that He hears us in whatever we ask, we know that we have the requests that we have asked of Him."
I John 5:14-15 (ESV)

Recently our church took part in Baptist Women's Day. During the service the various ladies' missions groups were highlighted, we had a special speaker, and ladies who don't normally take part in leading worship took part.

One of those ladies was me.

I had been asked to lead the morning prayer. I agreed and spent much time writing down my thoughts and making an outline of what I wanted to say in my prayers. I don't really mind public speaking but don't do it that often and still get a little nervous. I didn't want to embarrass myself.

When it came time to lead the prayer, I headed to the pulpit with my outline. After asking the congregation if there were other names we should add to the prayer list and dutifully writing them down, I said "Let us pray," bowed my head, and with the help of my outline and notes began to pray. I'm pretty sure I remembered all the names that had been added to the prayer list and didn't stumble too badly.

A few minutes later, it was time for the offering. The two children's missions groups were in charge of passing the offering plates during the service. One of the children said the offertory prayer. He is a first grader, the same age as my older daughter. He started his prayer, and after saying a few things, he paused and said, very emphatically "I KNOW YOU HEAR US!" Pretty soon after that, he said "Amen" and they passed the plates.

But you know what?

His prayer was *fantastic*. Sincere. No notes...no cheat sheet...no evidence he was worried that people would think he wasn't praying like he should. He was talking to his Friend.

Let me say that again.

He was talking to his Friend.

Talking with no pretense, no fluff, nothing but the utmost sincerity. And the absolute belief that his Friend...his Jesus...his Lord and Savior HEARS. Hears every single word.

I am certain that Jesus did.

This child demonstrated through his prayer such faith and such trust. His focus was on the prayer, on talking with Jesus and nothing else. He wasn't concerned that he was going to forget something he should have said, or that his prayer wasn't going to sound good. He was simply talking to Jesus in a pure and wonderful way.

He was the most sincere speaker of the day.

Even though the service was wonderful, I got the biggest blessing from his prayer...the biggest blessing and the best lesson.

Jesus wants to hear from us. Jesus wants to hear from him. Jesus wants to hear from me.

And I don't think Jesus cares if I don't sound eloquent...or if I stumble and fumble all over myself. I don't think He minds if sometimes I don't know what to say or even how to pray. When my brain is so fogged up with the things going on in my life and in the world and all I can manage to get out are a few incoherent thoughts.

The important thing to remember is to take some time to speak with Him each day. To speak and then be quiet and listen.

Like the little boy said that Sunday...

I know You hear us!

Questions? Comments? I would love to hear from you. Feel free to email me at tweakingsandtappings2@gmail.com

If you feel led, please leave a review at Amazon.com and be sure to check out my first book <u>Tweakings and Tappings: When God Gets My Attention</u> available at Amazon

Thank you,

Suzanne Wachs Jones